VELOCITY ETUDES

By William Bay

WBM11
ISBN 97809859227-8-8

WILLIAM
BAY**MUSIC**

Visit us on the Web at www.williambaymusic.com

Preface

Velocity Etudes is a collection of 43 original compositions designed to enhance important elements of classic guitar technique. I have always felt that as important as scale and technique drills are, they can by themselves be very tedious to practice. In addition, technique has relevance only in the context of the entire musical composition it is intended to enhance. For example, think of a football player who is excellent in doing a particular calisthenic drill but who cannot "put it all together" in the context of a competitive game. So I like to present technique as part of a musical composition. These etudes were composed with this thought in mind.

The compositions can be used merely as technical studies but they also may be used as short concert or recital pieces. Several of them may be grouped to present a kind of suite. I hope you enjoy playing these etudes. The guitar has so many moods and colors. Good technique enables the guitarist to bring out the breadth and subtlety of expression possible with this instrument. I have tried to present a variety of moods, rhythms and textures in these compositions and have presented a workable assortment of keys, both major and minor.

Other books, compositions and recordings in the *William Bay Music* catalog are available on my website: *williambaymusic.com*

William Bay

Contents

Etude 1 in A Major

William Bay

4

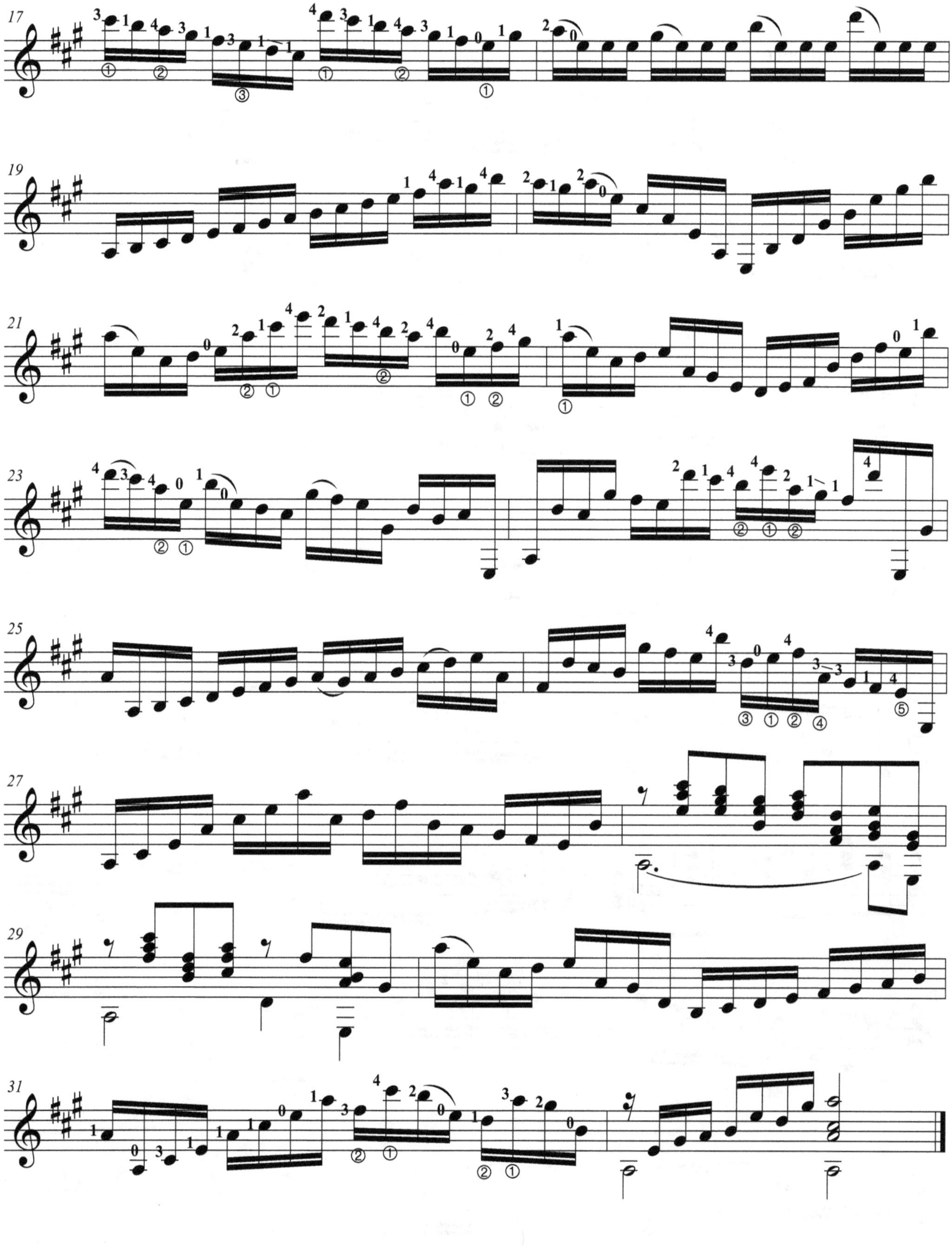
17
19
21
23
25
27
29
31

Etude 2 in A minor

William Bay

6

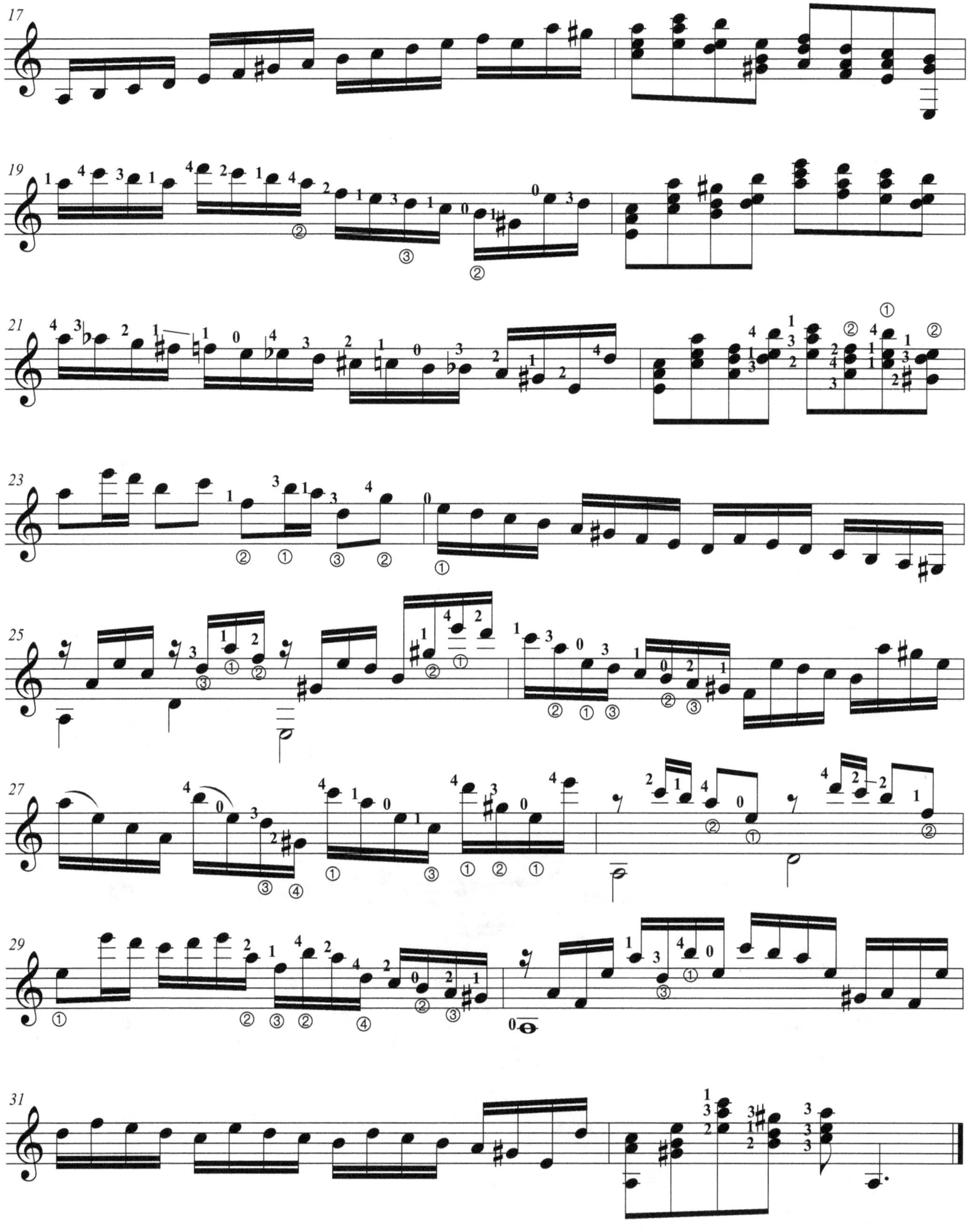
17
19
21
23
25
27
29
31

Etude 3 in E minor

William Bay

Allegro ♩ = 88

8

This page has been left blank
to avoid awkward page turns.

Etude 4 in D Major

William Bay

Moderato ♩ = 100

Guitar

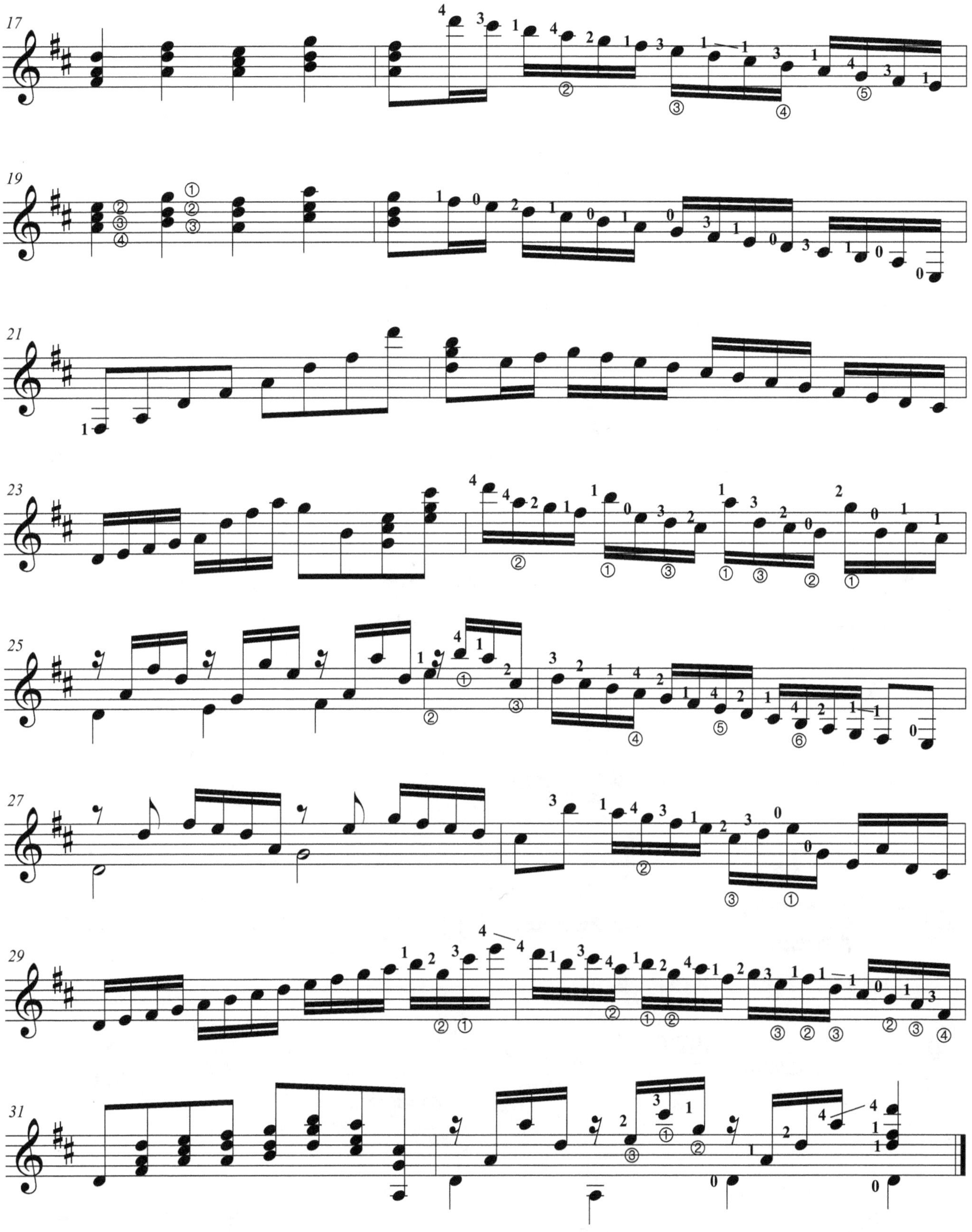

Etude 5 in E Major

William Bay

Allegro ♩ = 92

Barre II

Etude 6 in C Major

William Bay

Allegro ♩ = 84

14

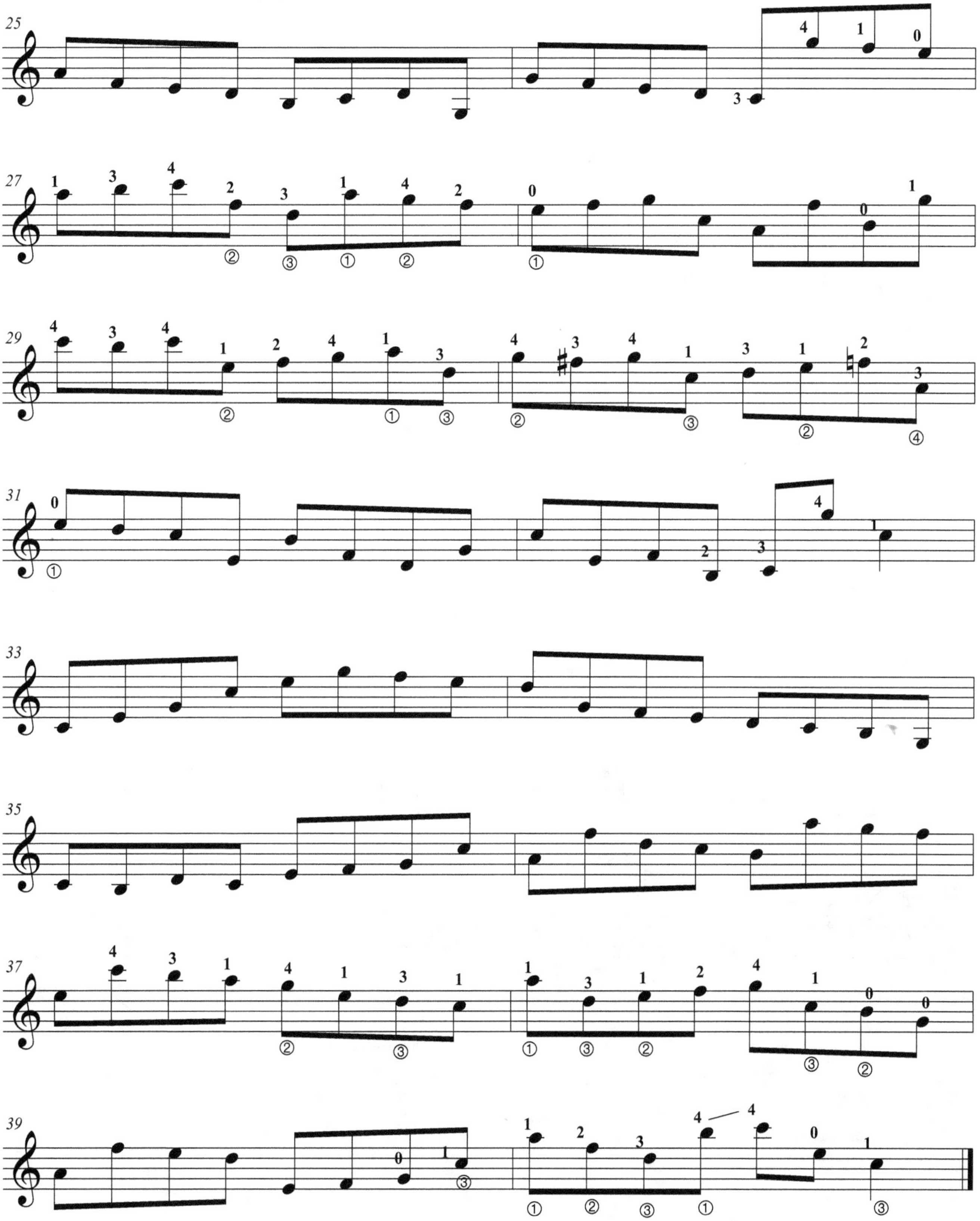

Etude 7 in A minor

William Bay

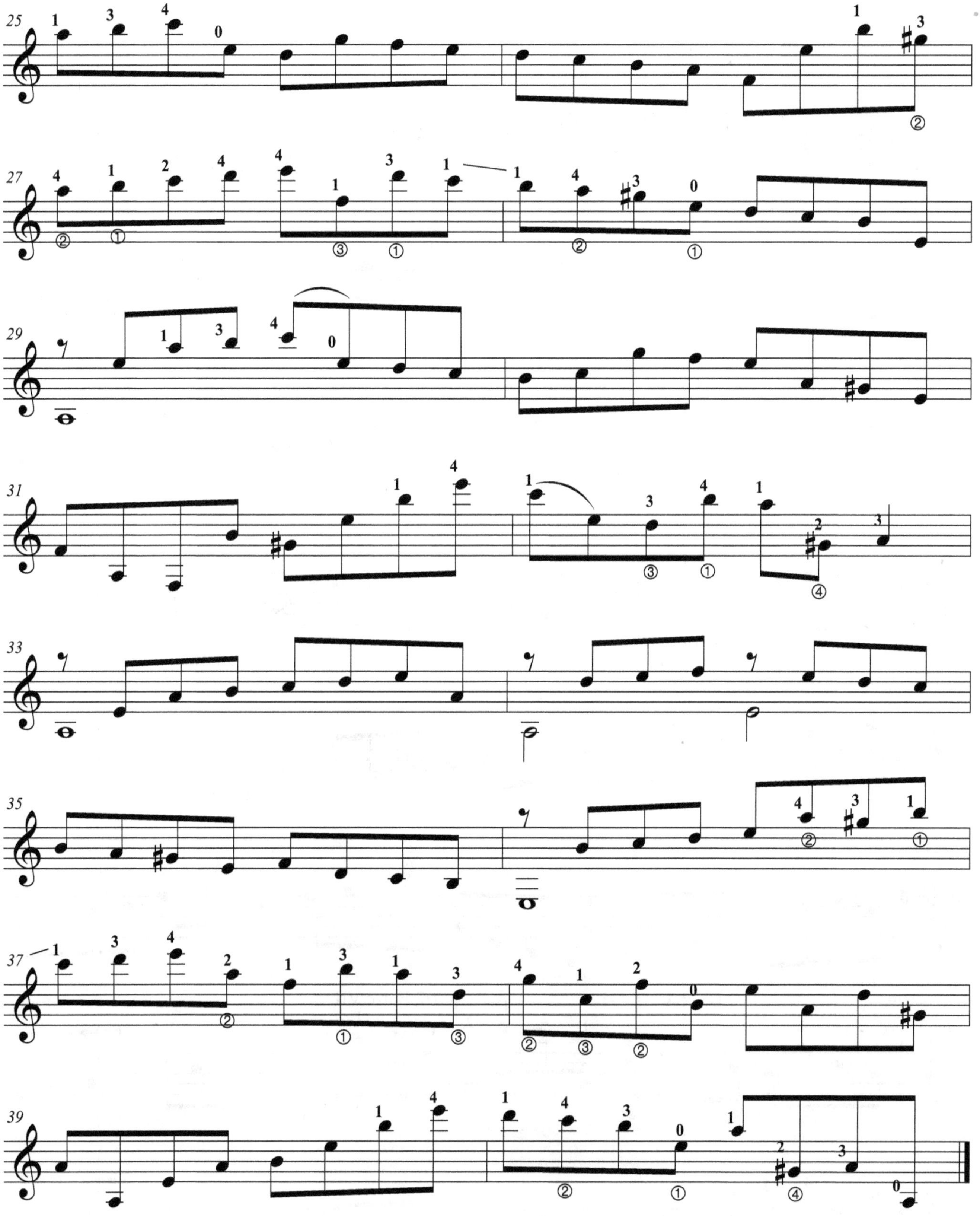

Etude 8 in G Major

William Bay

18

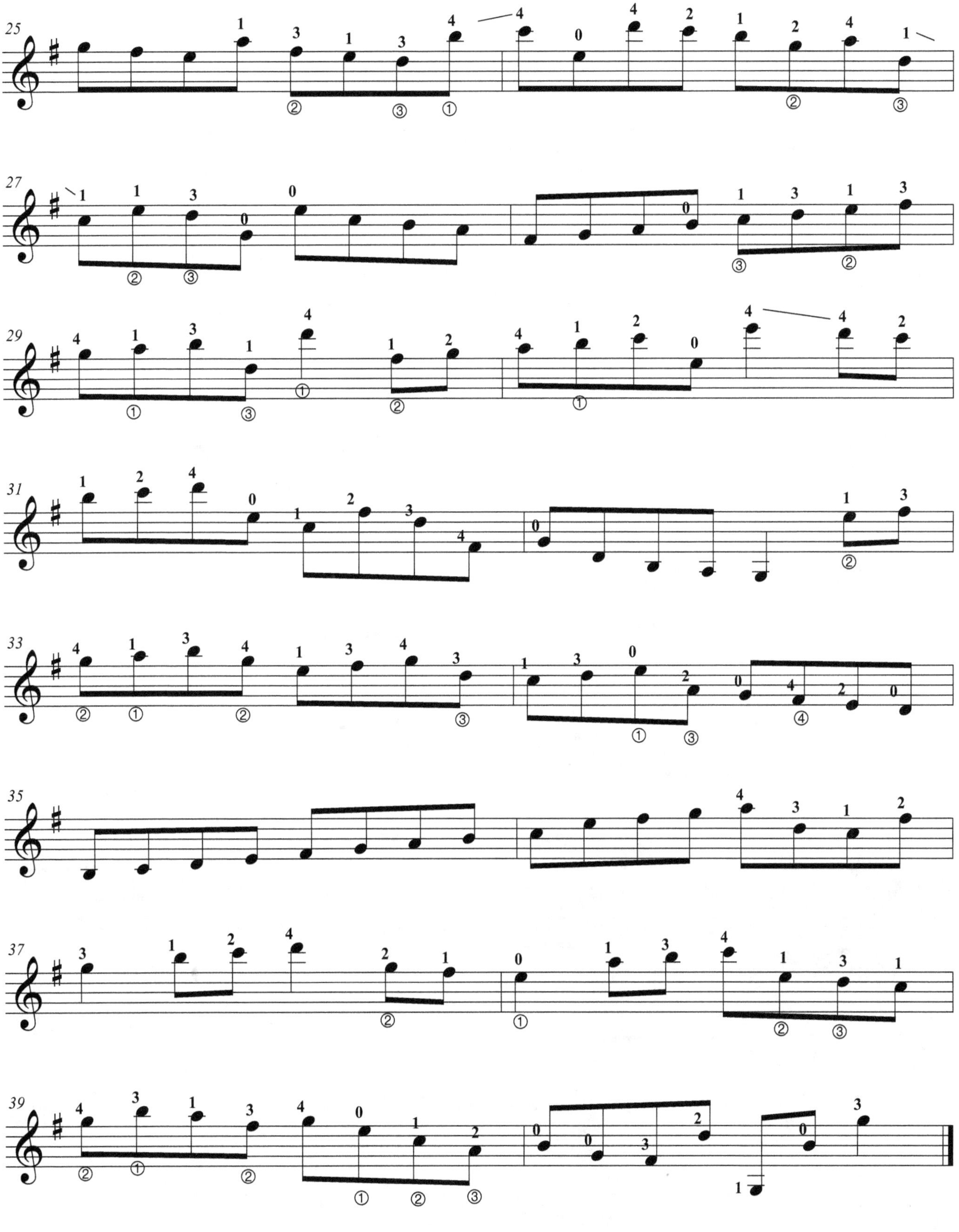

Etude 9 in B minor

William Bay

20

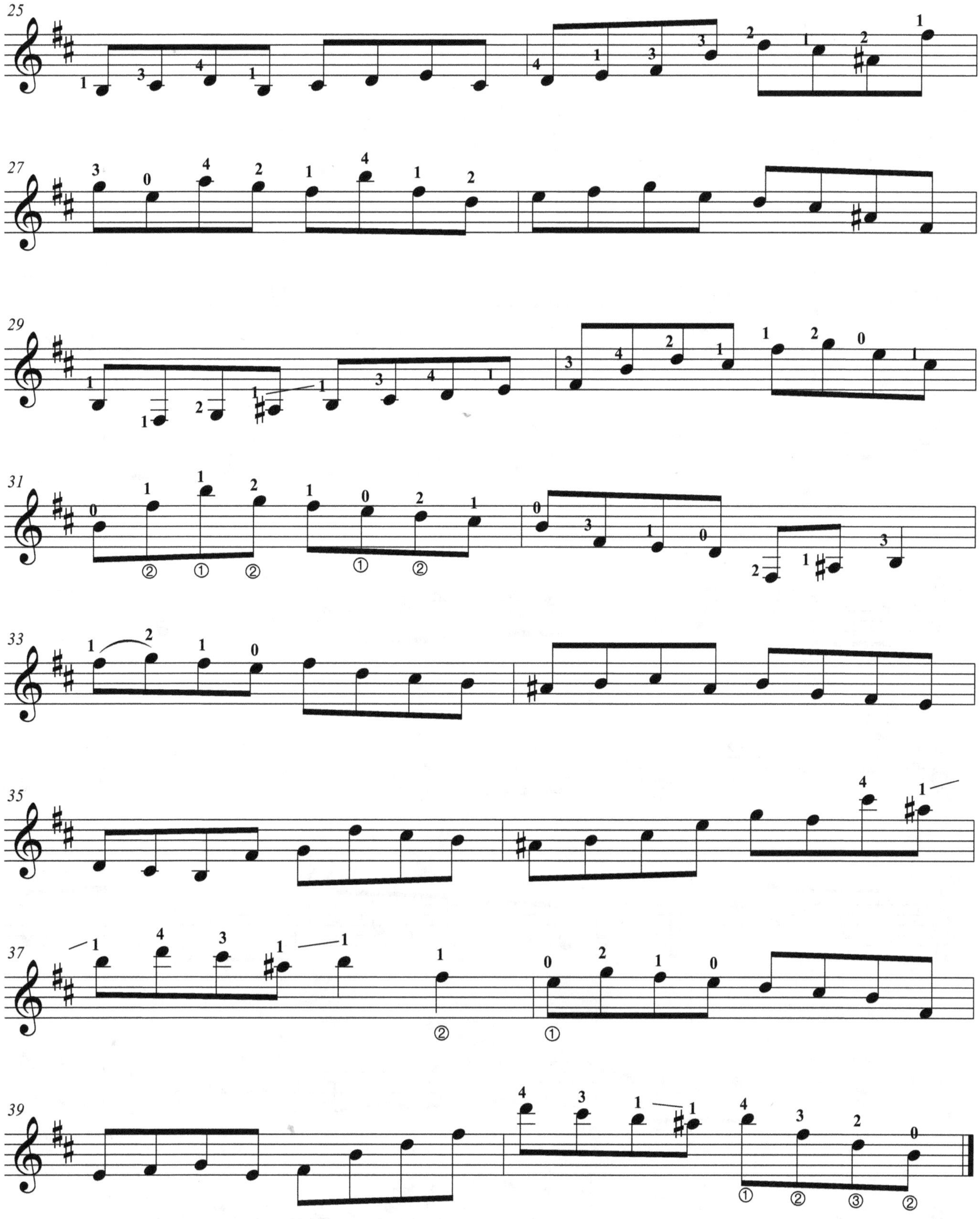

Etude 10 in F Major

Presto ♩ = 98

William Bay

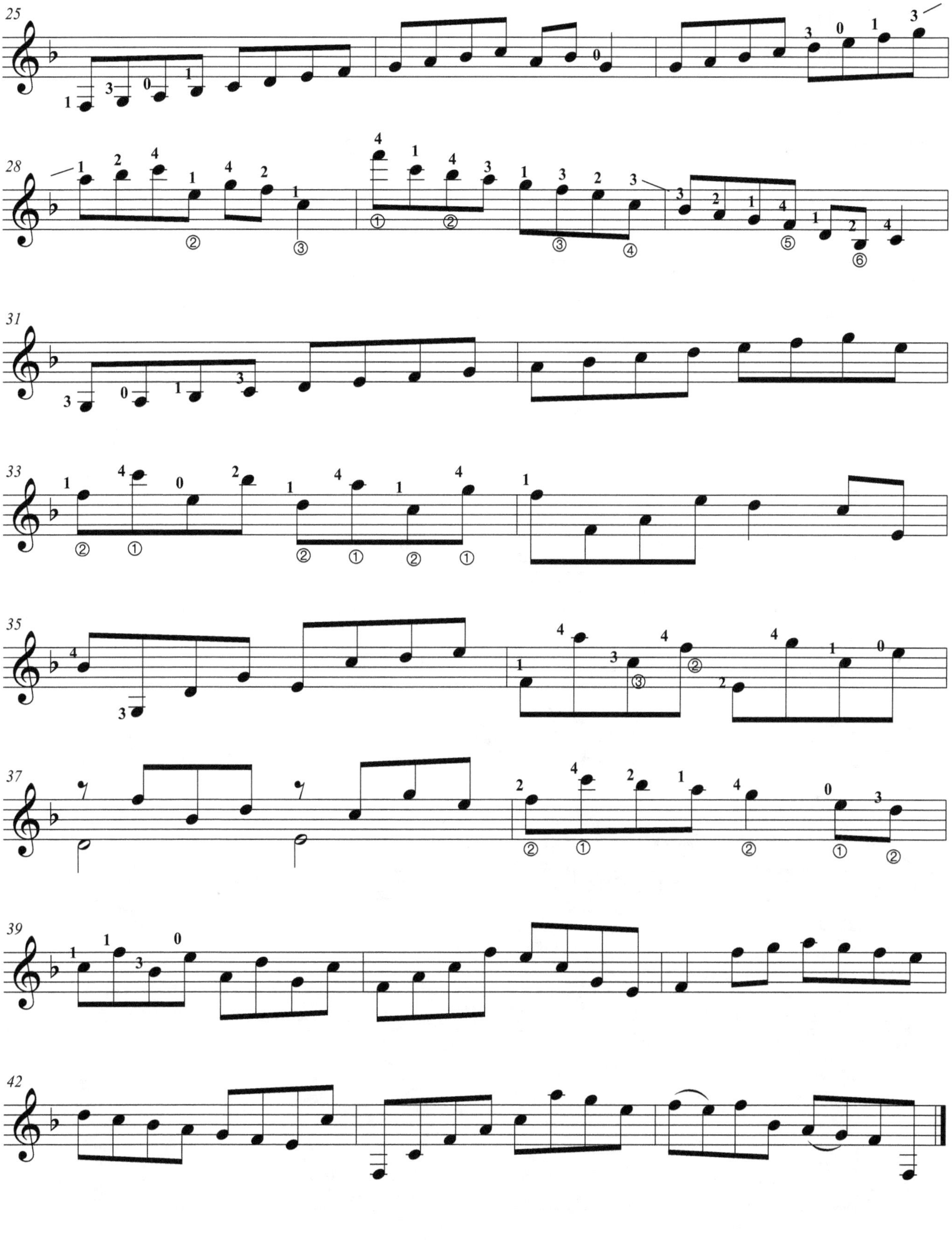

Etude 11 in D minor

Dropped D Tuning

William Bay

Allegro ♩ = 78

24

Etude 12 in C Sharp minor

William Bay

Allegro ♩ = 74

Etude 13 in A Major

William Bay

Allegro ♩ = 84

This page has been left blank
to avoid awkward page turns.

Etude 14 in D minor

Dropped D Tuning

William Bay

28

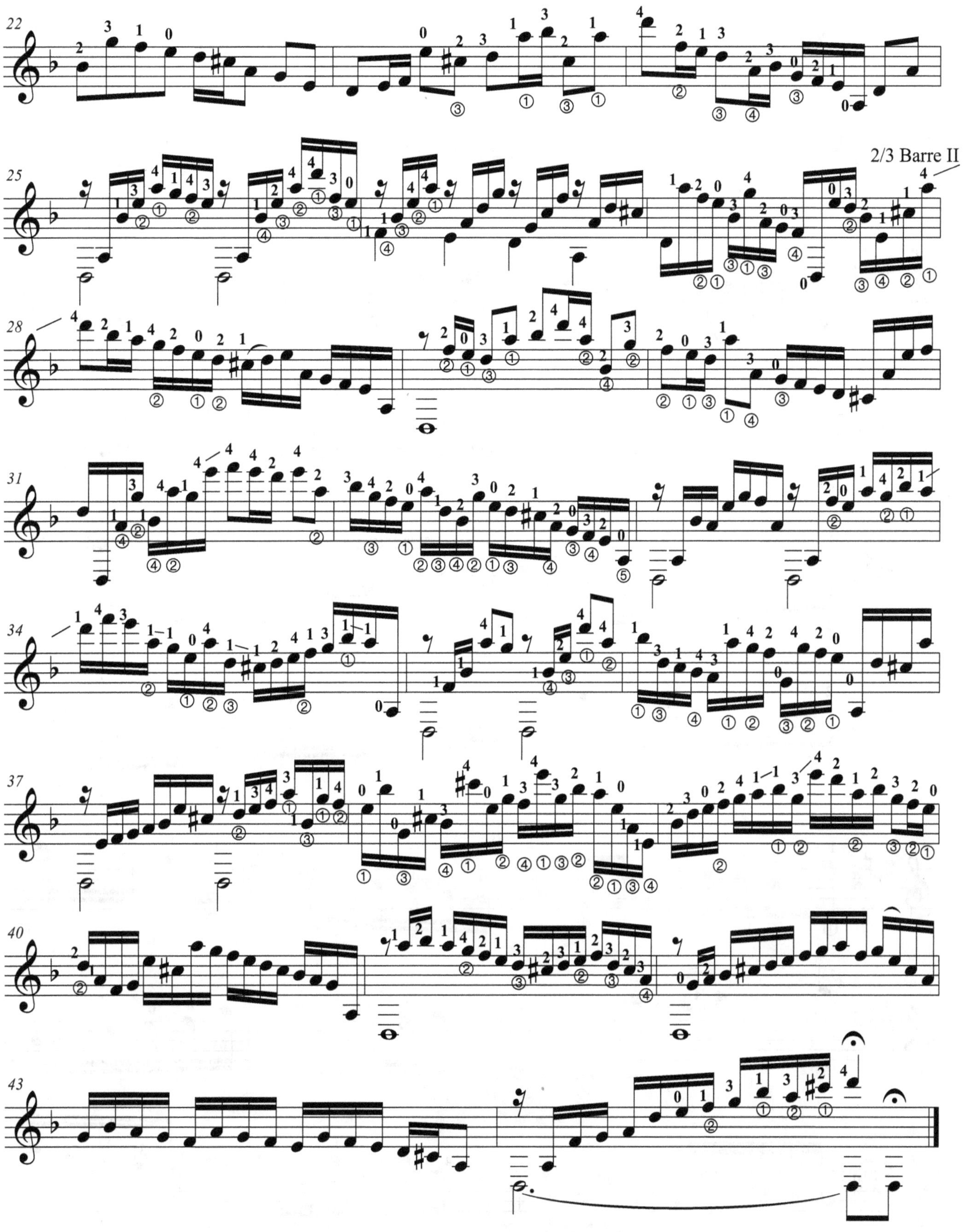
2/3 Barre II

Etude 15 in E Major

William Bay

Vivace ♪ = 192

30

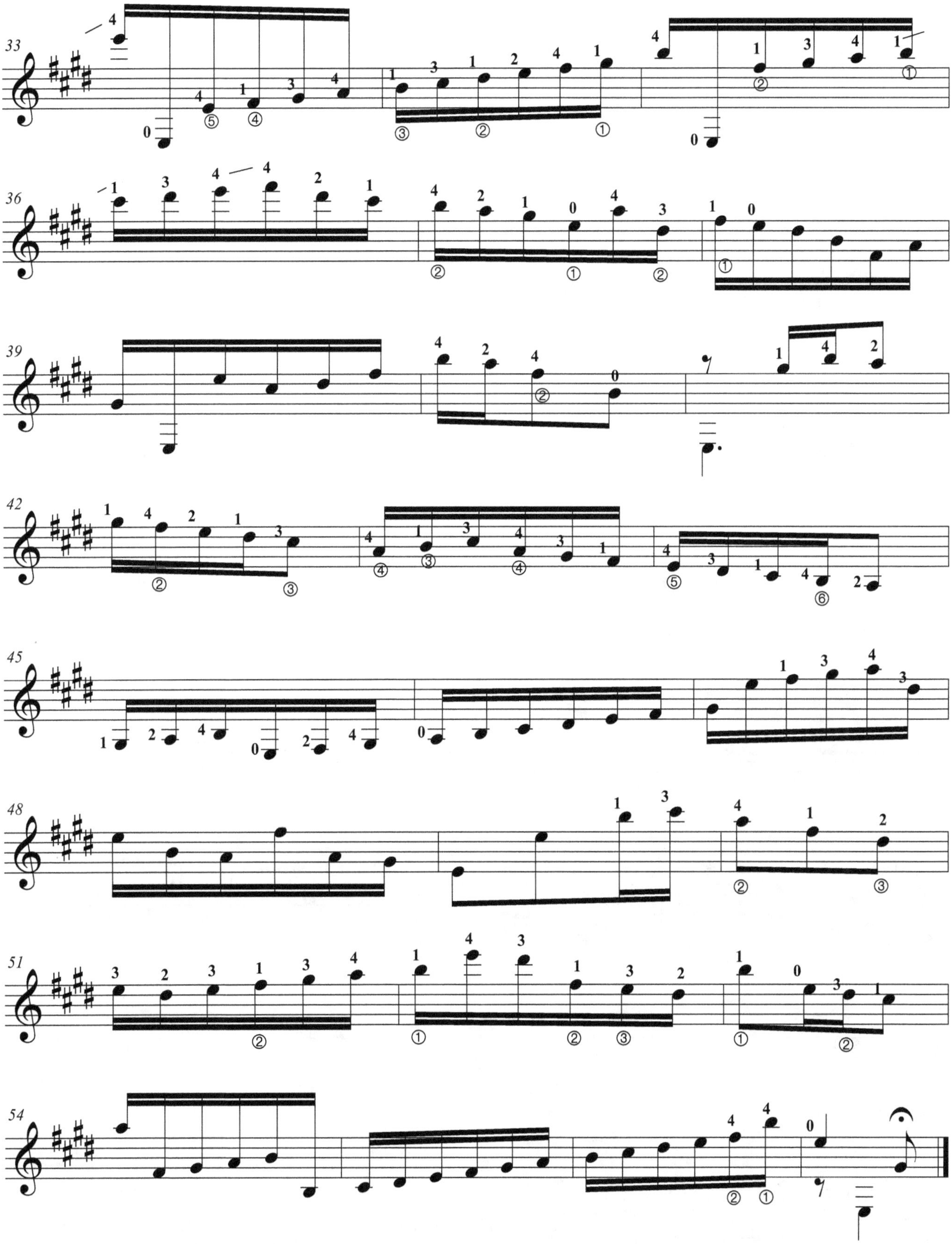

Etude 16 in C Major

William Bay

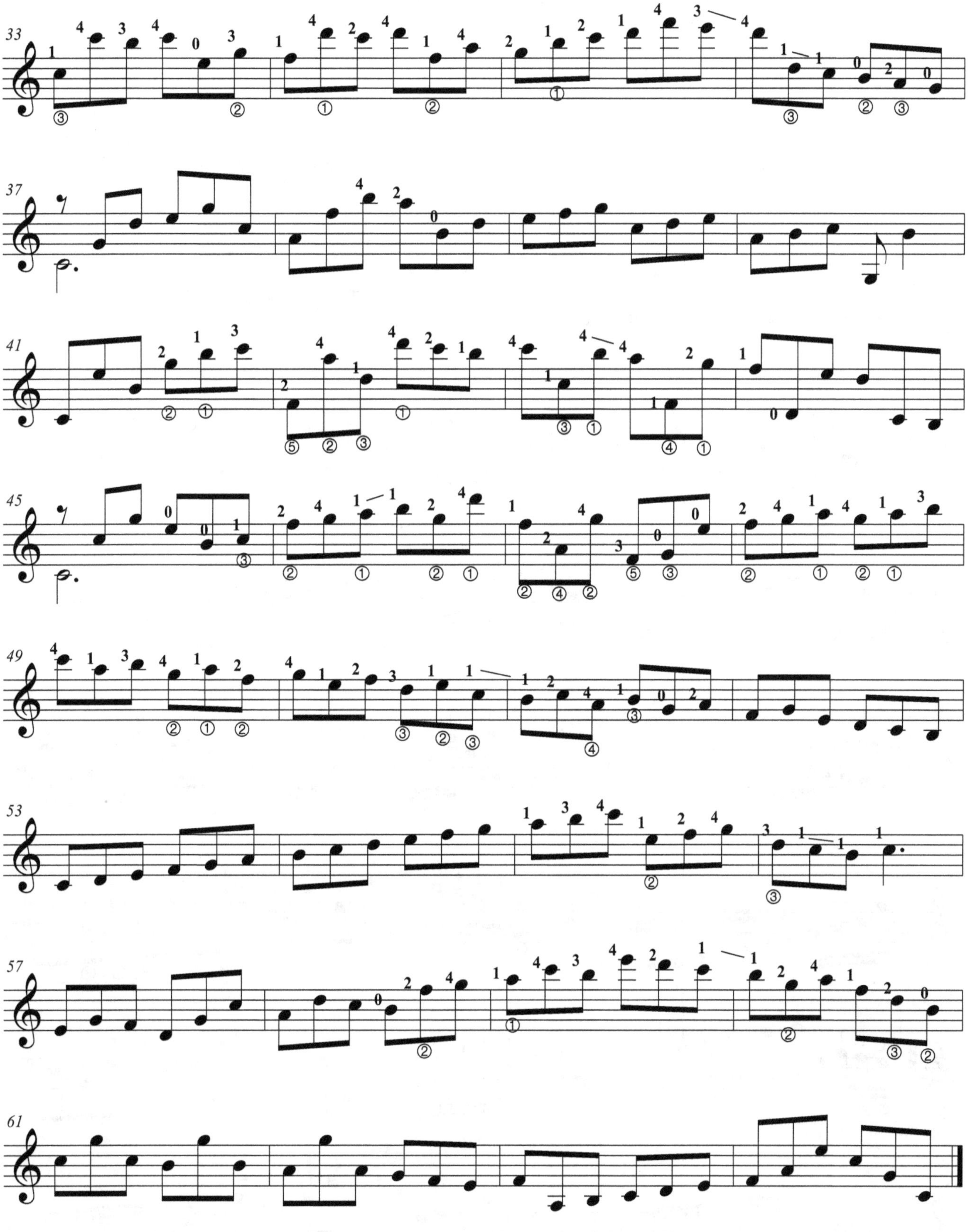

Etude 17 in E minor

William Bay

Allegro ♩ = 96

This page has been left blank
to avoid awkward page turns.

Etude 18 in B minor

Moderato ♩ = 160

William Bay

36

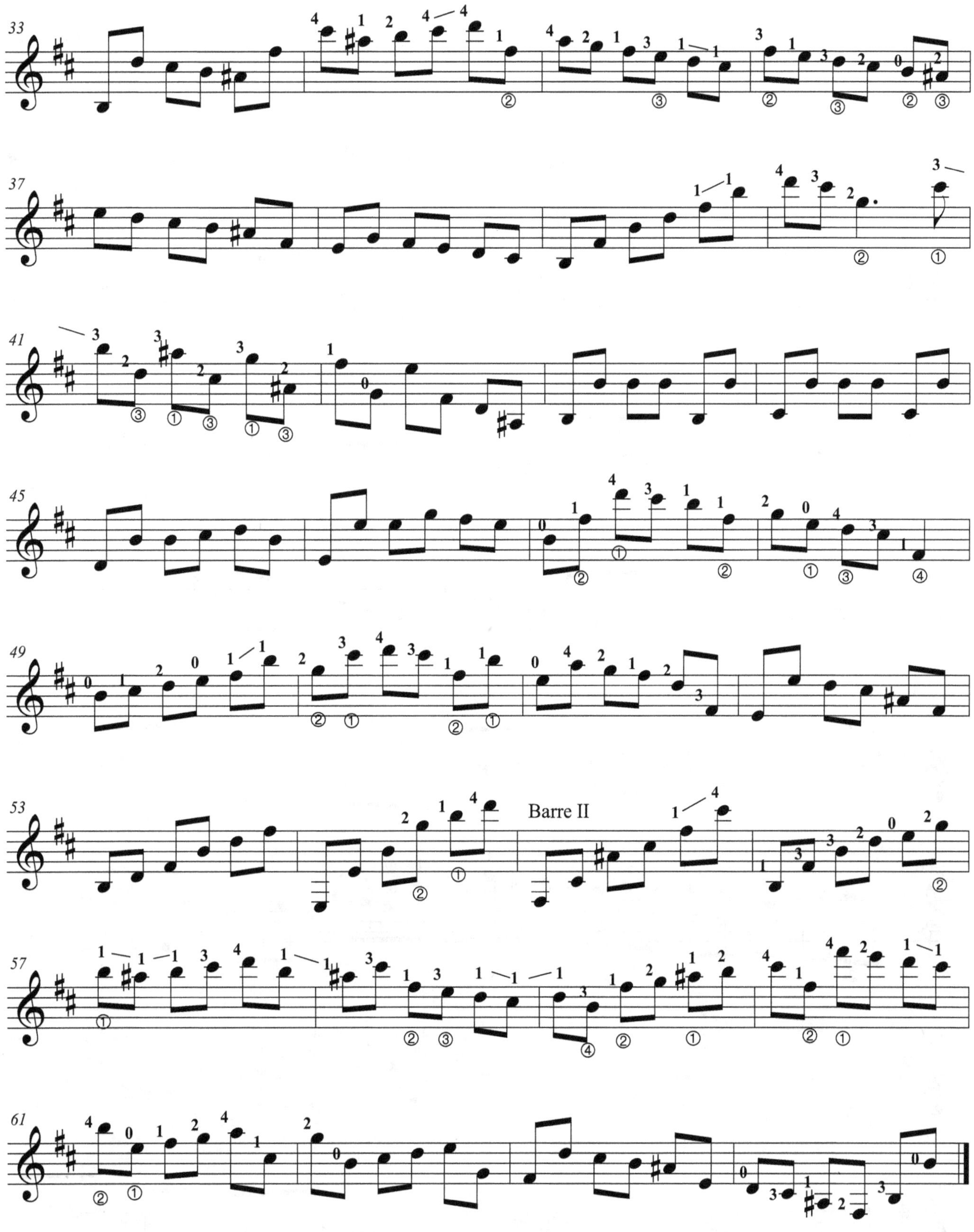
Barre II

Etude 19 in G Major

William Bay

Allegro ♩ = 76

Guitar

mf

This page has been left blank
to avoid awkward page turns.

Etude 20 in A minor

William Bay

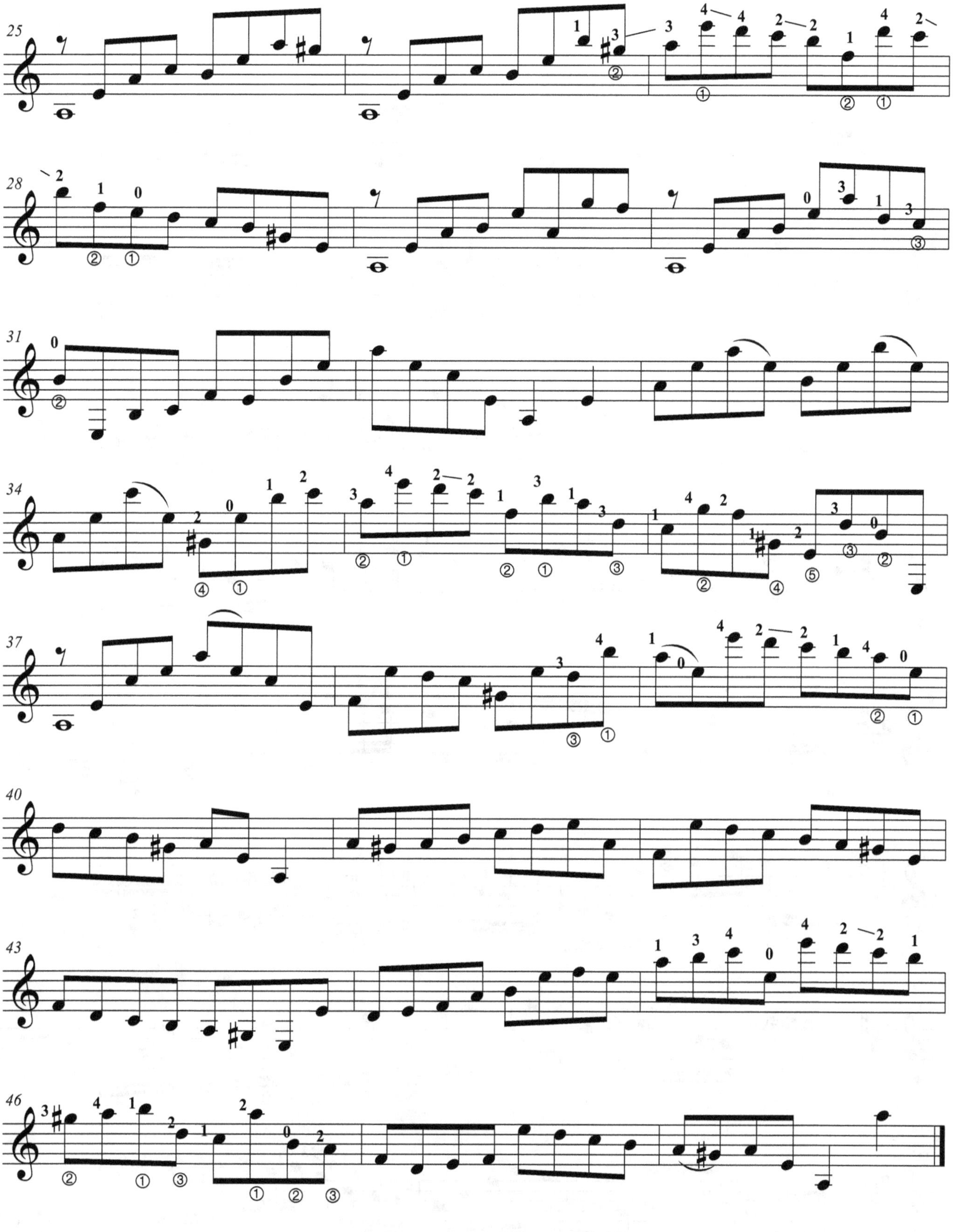
25
28
31
34
37
40
43
46

Etude 21 in F sharp minor

William Bay

Moderato ♩ = 70

Guitar

mf

This page has been left blank
to avoid awkward page turns.

Etude 22 in D minor

Dropped D Tuning

William Bay

Allegretto ♩ = 100

Guitar

© 2013 by William Bay. All Rights Reserved. BMI.

44

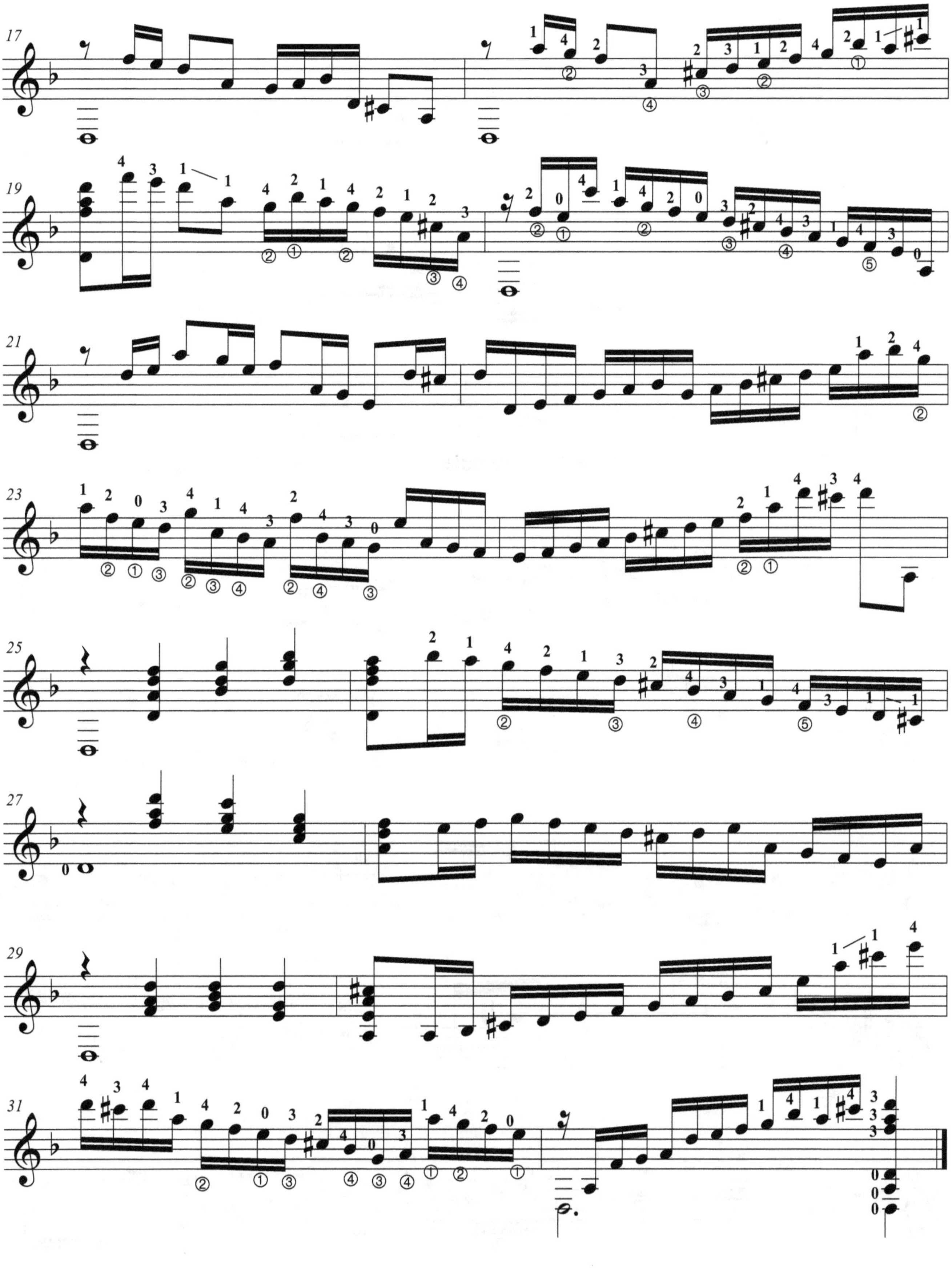

Etude 23 in E Major

Moderato ♩ = 88

William Bay

46

47

Etude 24 in A minor

William Bay

Presto ♪ = 168

Guitar

48

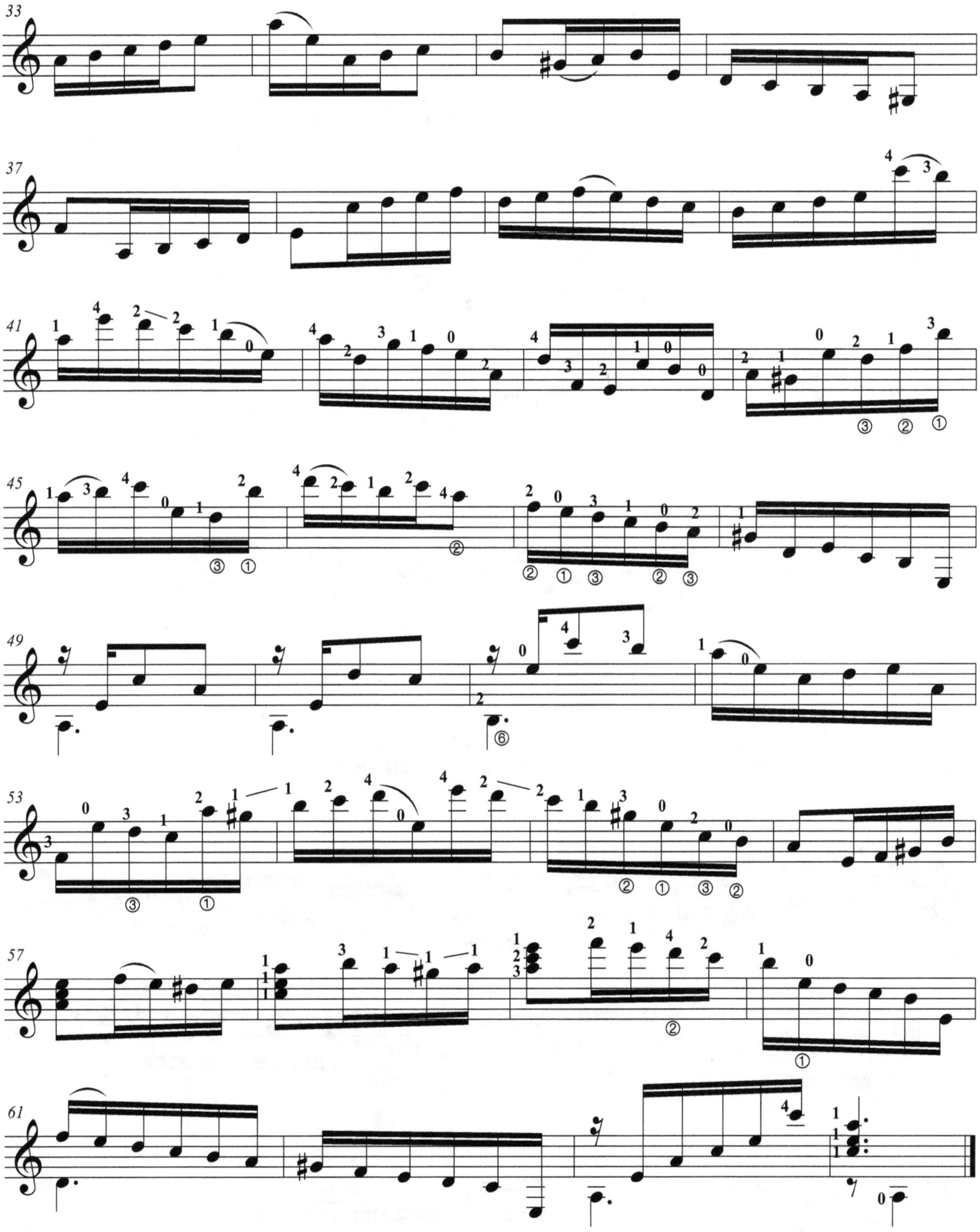

Etude 25 in A Major

William Bay

51

Etude 26 in D Major

Dropped D Tuning

William Bay

Moderato ♩ = 86

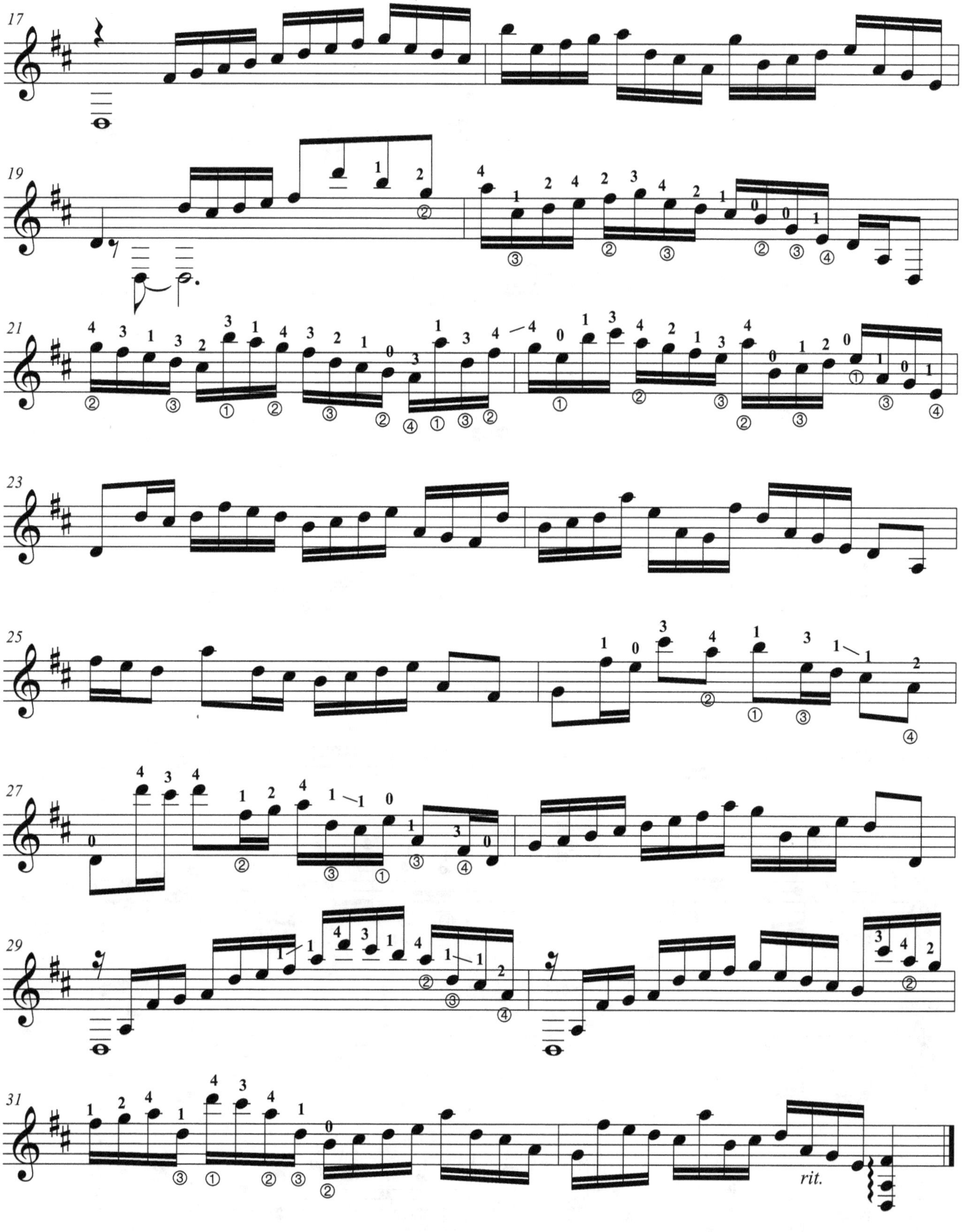
17
19
21
23
25
27
29
31
rit.

Etude 27 in E minor

William Bay

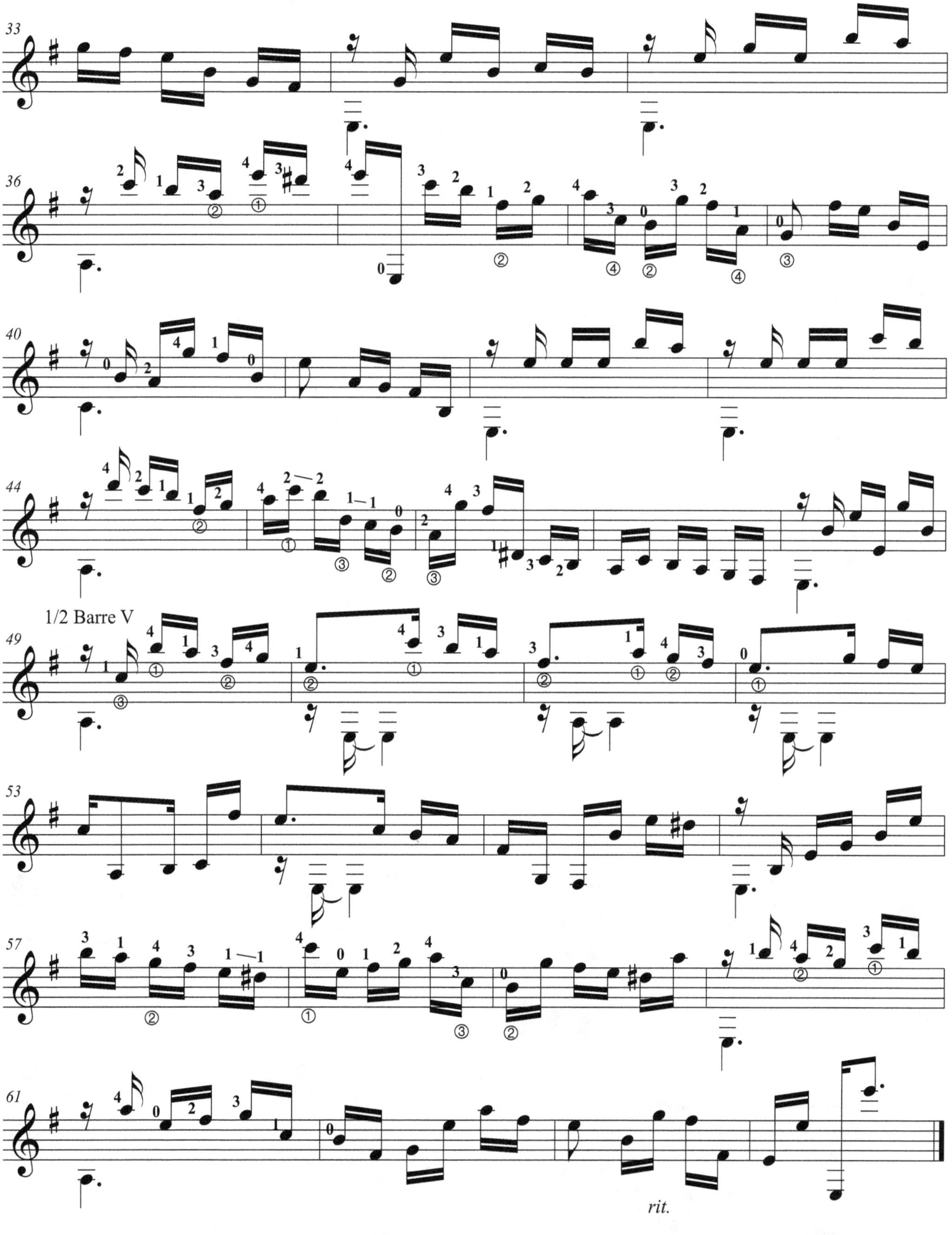
1/2 Barre V
rit.

Etude 28 in G Major

William Bay

Moderato ♩ = 90

Guitar

56

This page has been left blank
to avoid awkward page turns.

Etude 29 in C minor

William Bay

Allegro ♩ = 92

1/2 Barre VIII

5/6 Barre III
Barre I
5/6 Barre III
5/6 Barre III
Barre I
5/6 Barre III

Etude 30 in A minor

William Bay

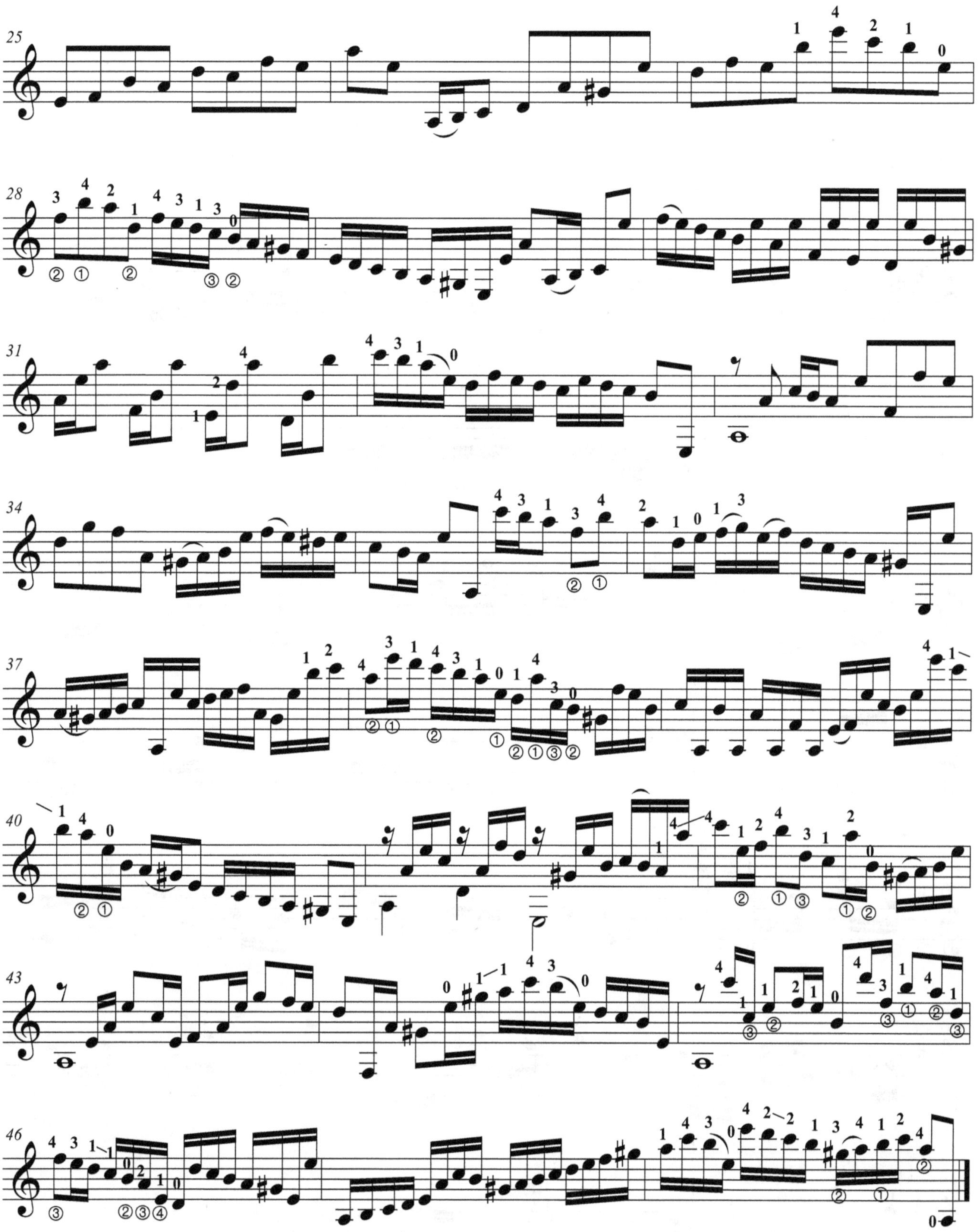

Etude 31 in E minor

William Bay

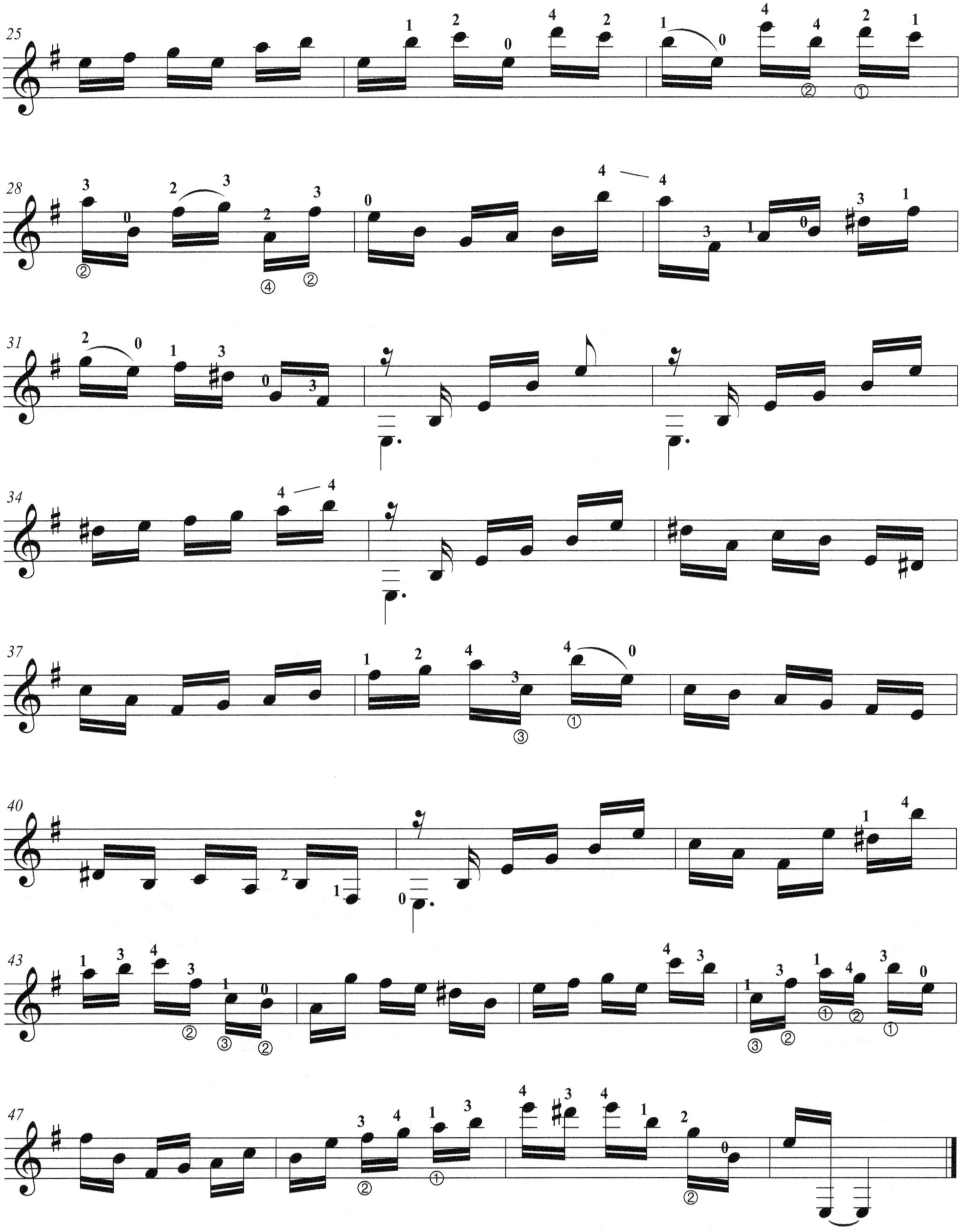

Etude 32 in A minor

William Bay

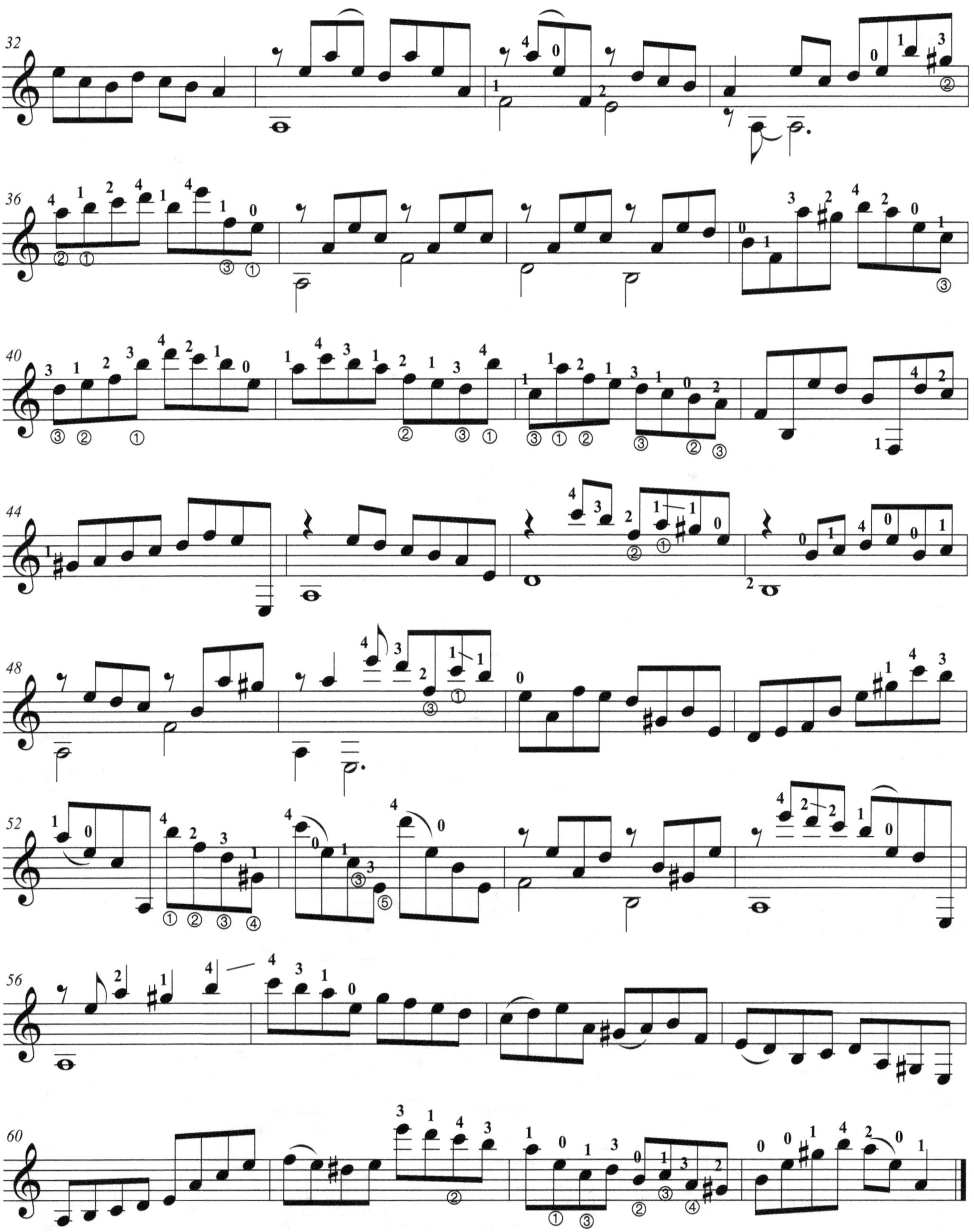

Etude 33 in D Major

Dropped D Tuning

William Bay

Allegro ♩ = 86

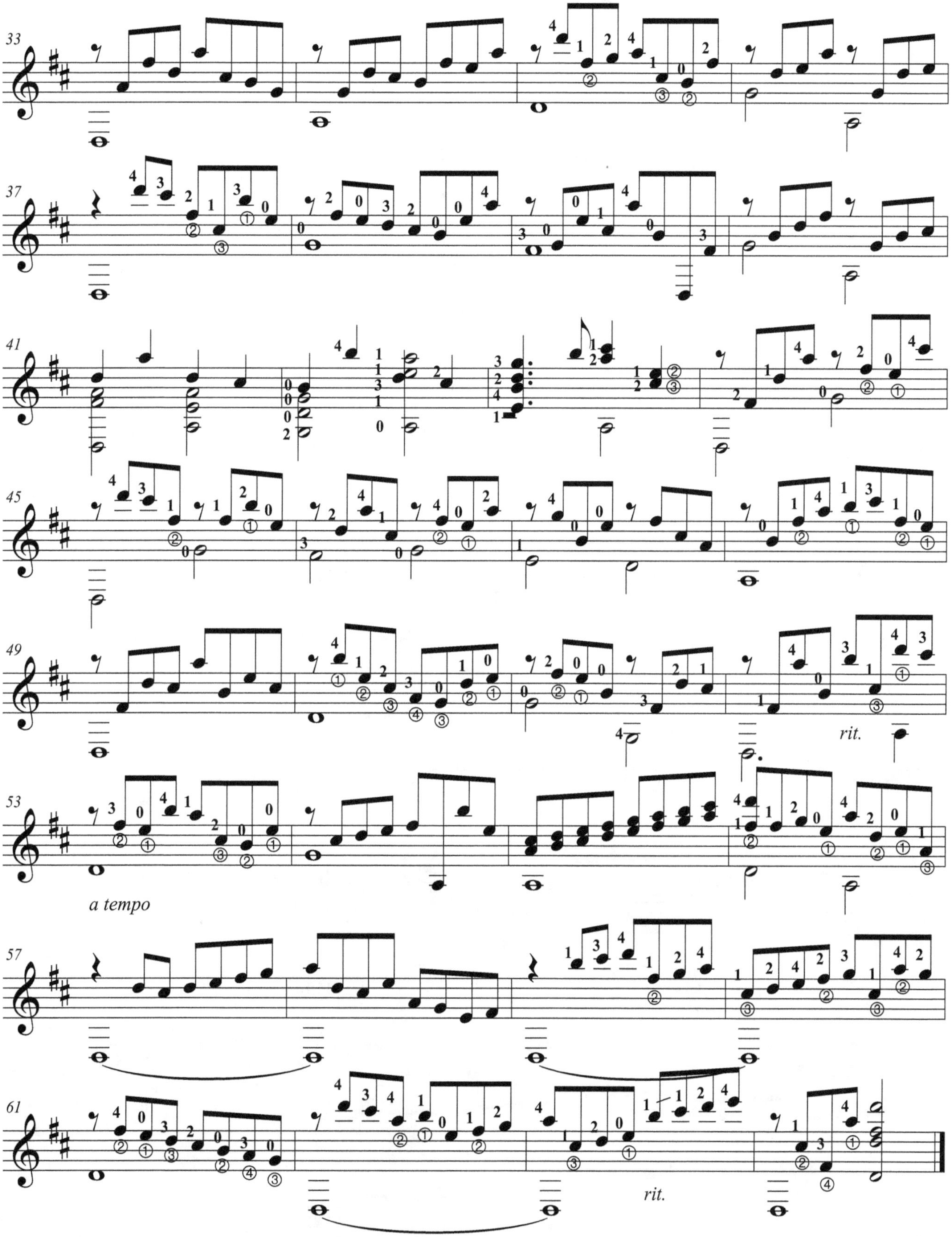
rit.
a tempo
rit.

Etude 34 in C Major

William Bay

Allegro ♩ = 92

1/2 Barre VII

© 2013 by William Bay. All Rights Reserved. BMI.

68

This page has been left blank
to avoid awkward page turns.

Etude 35 in D minor

Dropped D Tuning

Allegretto ♩ = 120

William Bay

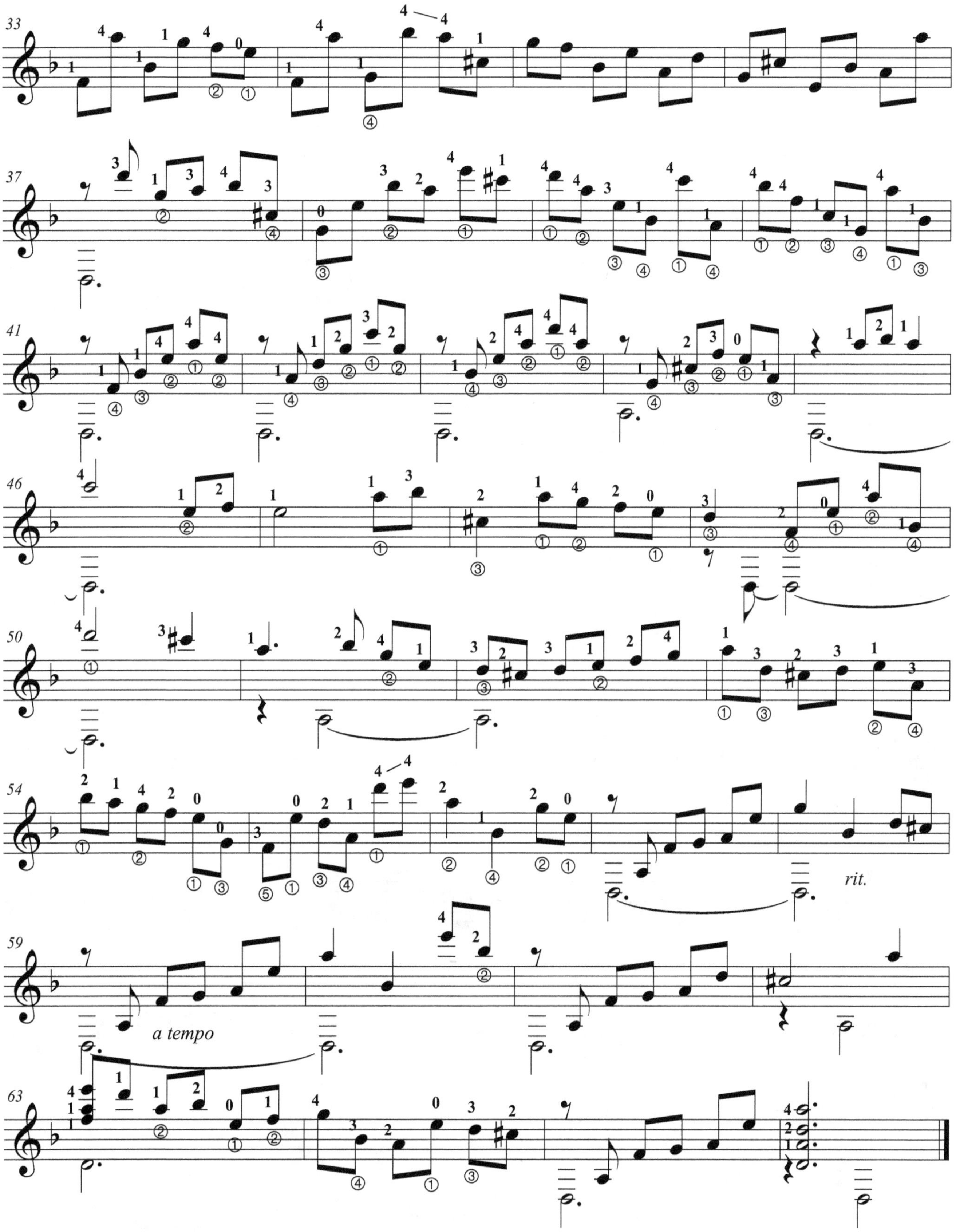
rit.
a tempo

Etude 36 in A Major

William Bay

This page has been left blank
to avoid awkward page turns.

Etude 37 in B minor

William Bay

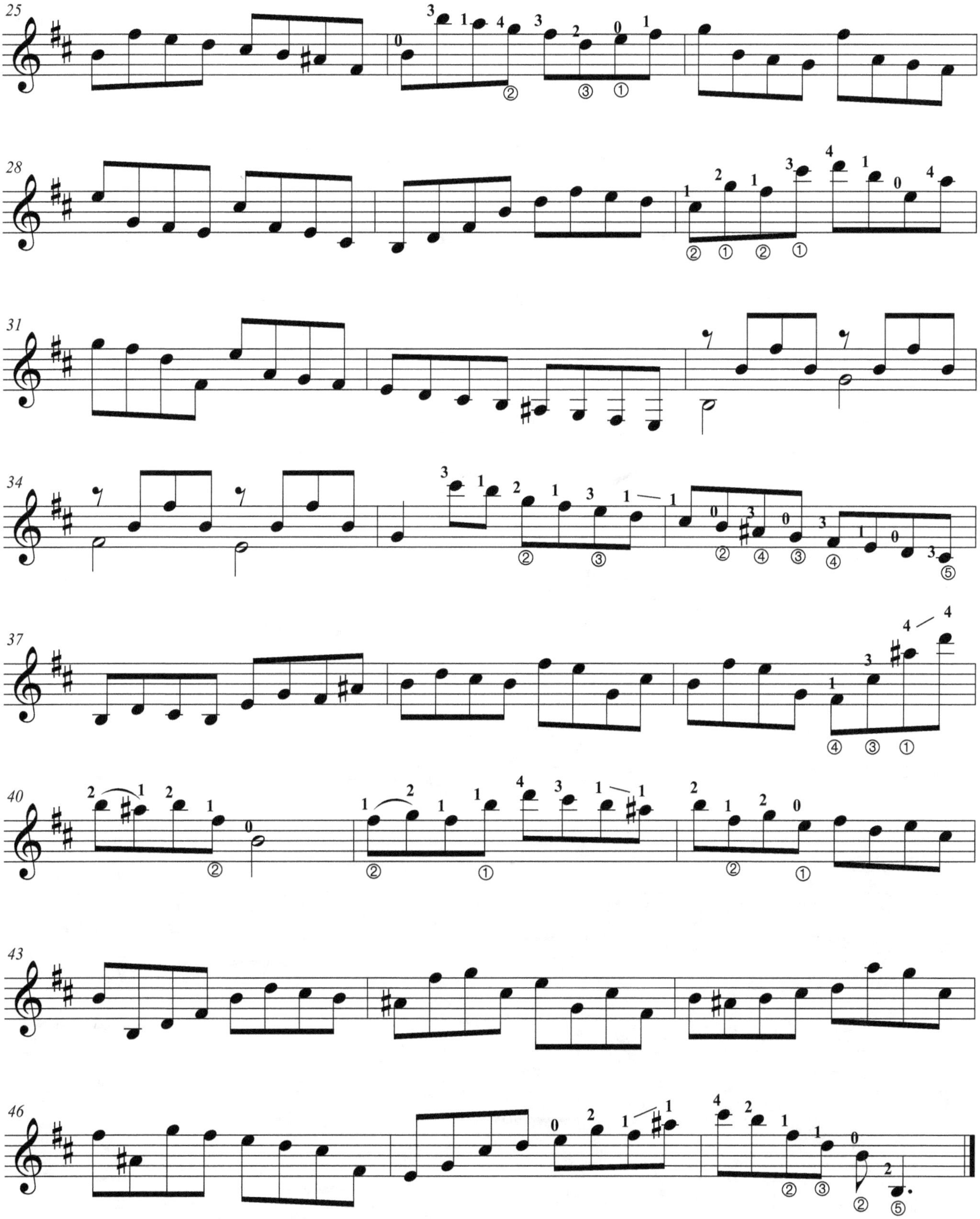

Etude 38 in G Major

William Bay

Moderato ♩ = 80

Guitar

1/2 Barre V

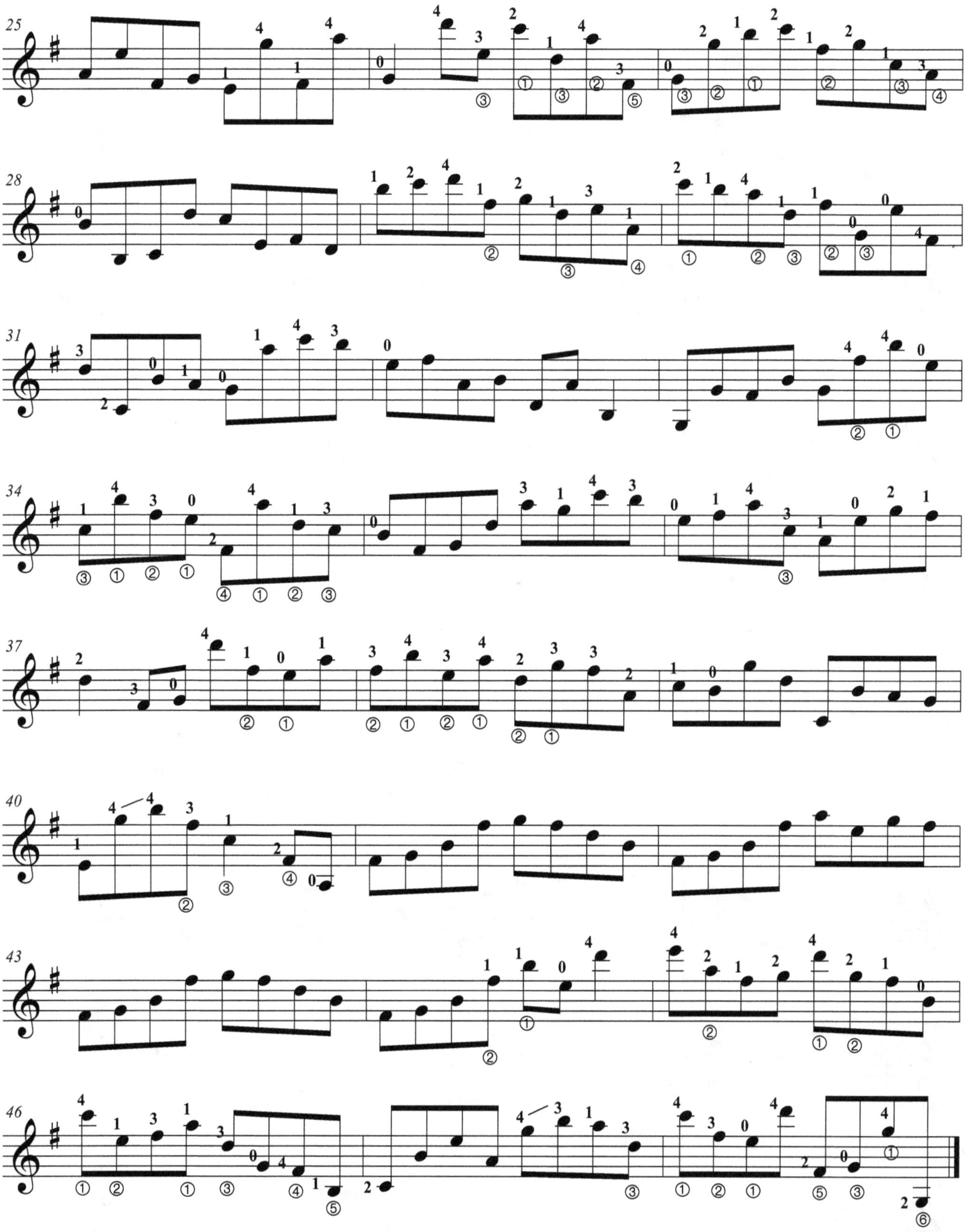

Etude 39 in F sharp minor

William Bay

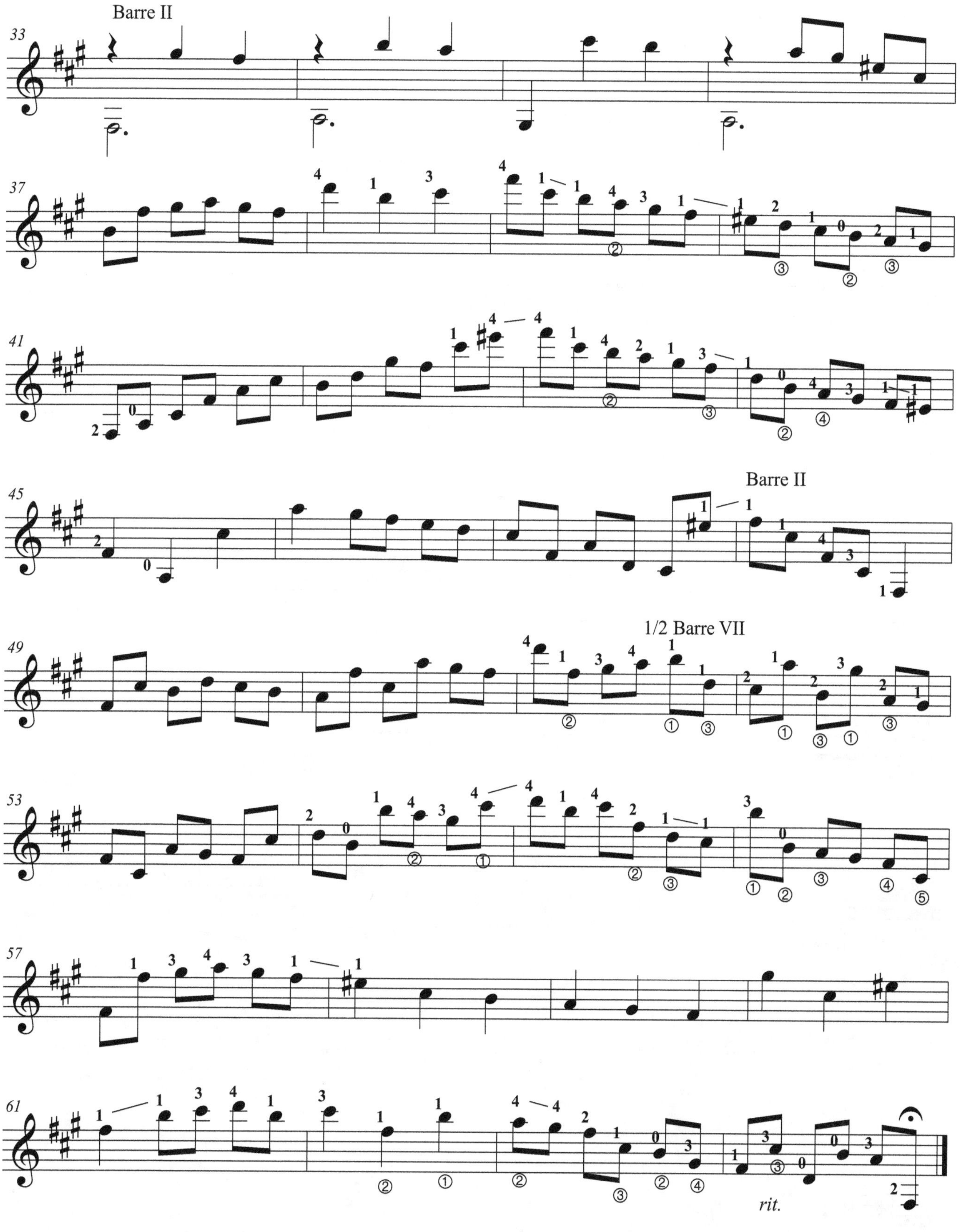
Barre II
Barre II
1/2 Barre VII
rit.

Etude 40 in B minor

William Bay

Etude 41 in C Major

William Bay

Etude 42 in E minor

William Bay

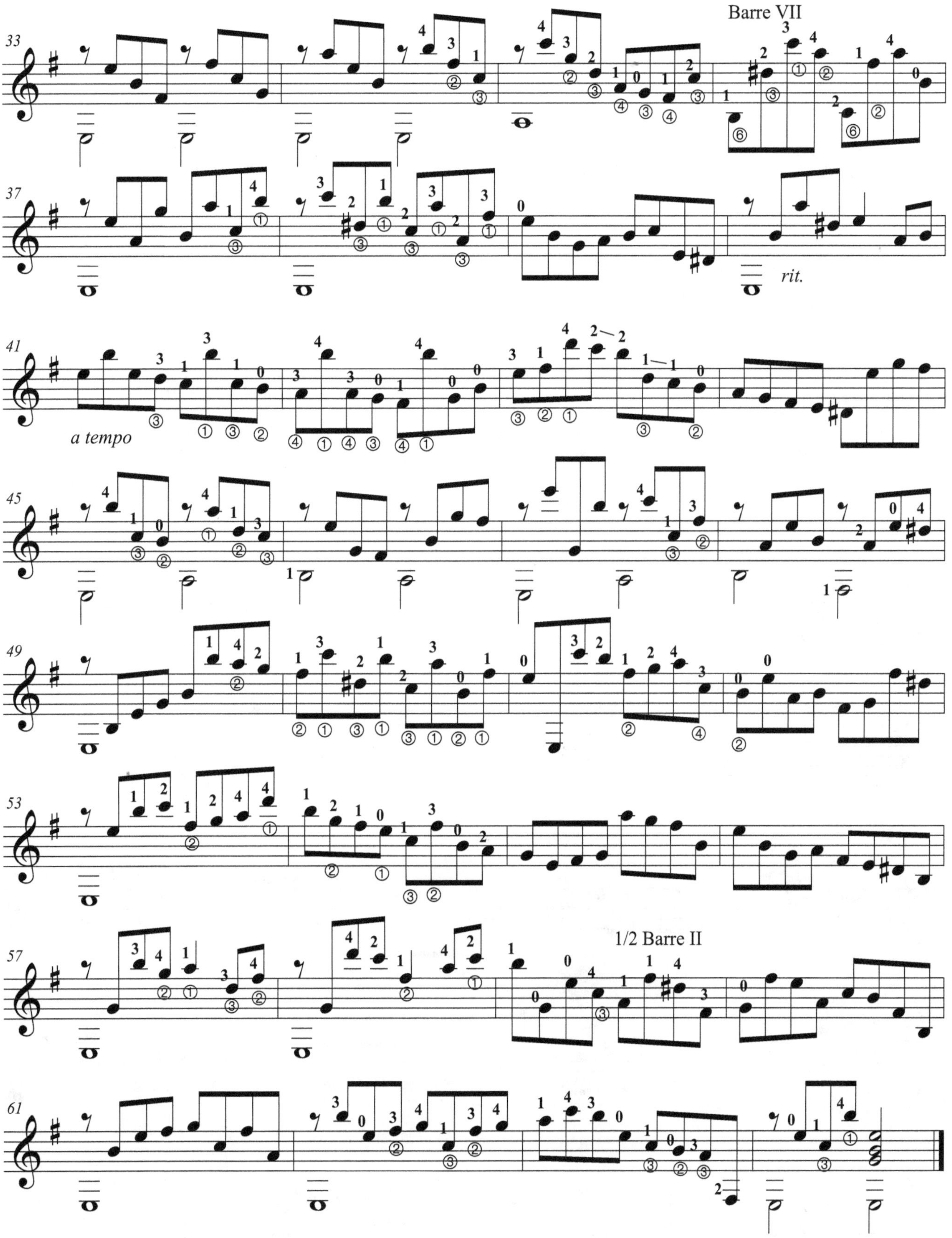
Barre VII
a tempo
rit.
1/2 Barre II

Etude 43 in A minor

William Bay

www.ingramcontent.com/pod-product-compliance
Lightning Source LLC
Chambersburg PA
CBHW062052090426
42740CB00016B/3109